Word Work

Short Vowel Sounds in VCCV Pattern

15 min.

You will need
- Teacher-made word cards
- paper
- pencil

● Choose five word cards from those provided by your teacher. Write the words in a list. Quietly say each word aloud.

▲ Choose seven word cards from those provided by your teacher and write the words. Say each word aloud. Think of other words with these sounds. Add them to the list.

■ Choose nine word cards from those provided by your teacher and write the words. Make a five-column chart with the vowels *a, e, i, o, u* as headings. Write your words in the correct column.

Word Work

Suffixes *-ful, -ly,* and *-ion*

15 min.

You will need
- Teacher-made word cards
- paper
- pencil

● Choose four word cards from those provided by your teacher. Write the words. Say each word. Next to each word, write the base word. Write sentences for each word and base word that show the different meanings.

▲ Choose six word cards from those provided by your teacher and write the words. Say each word. Write sentences for each word and its base word. Notice how the suffixes change word meanings.

■ Choose twelve word cards from those provided by your teacher. Write the words. Say each word. Write sentences for each word and its base word. Notice how the suffixes change word meanings.

Grade 4, Unit 6, Week 5

Word Work

Short Vowel Sounds VCCV

You will need

15 min.

- Teacher-made word cards • paper • pencil

● Choose six word cards from those provided by your teacher. Write the words. Say each word. Think of other words you know with these short vowel sounds. Add the words to your list.

▲ Choose eight word cards from those provided by your teacher and write the words. Say each word. Think of other words you know with these short vowel sounds. Add them to your list.

■ Choose ten word cards from those provided by your teacher and write the words. Say each word. Make a five-column chart with short vowel sounds as headings. Write the words in the correct column.

Word Work

Suffixes -*less*, -*ment*, and -*ness*

15 min.

You will need
- Teacher-made word cards
- paper
- pencil

● Choose four word cards from those provided by your teacher. Write the words. Say each word. Next to each word, write the base word. Write sentences for each word and base word that show the different meanings.

▲ Choose six word cards from those provided by your teacher and write the words. Say each word. Write sentences for each word and its base word. Notice how the suffixes change word meanings.

■ Choose twelve word cards from those provided by your teacher. Write the words. Say each word. Write sentences for each word and its base word. Notice how the suffixes change word meanings.

Word Work

Words with Long *a* and Long *i* vowels

15 min.

You will need
- Teacher-made word cards
- paper
- pencil

● Choose six word cards from those provided by your teacher. Say each word. Make a two-column chart with headings *Long a* and *Long i*. Write each word in the correct column.

▲ Choose ten word cards from those provided by your teacher and say each word. Make a two-column chart with headings *Long a* and *Long i*. Write each word in the correct column.

■ Choose twelve word cards from those provided by your teacher. Group your words by long vowel sounds. Write each group in a list. Say each word. Add other words with these long vowel sounds to the lists.

Word Work

Prefixes *mis-*, *non-*, and *re-*

15 min.

You will need
- Teacher-made word cards
- paper
- pencil

● Choose four word cards from those provided by your teacher. Write the words. Say each word. Next to each word, write the base word. Write sentences for each word and base word that show the different meanings.

▲ Choose six word cards from those provided by your teacher and write the words. Say each word. Write sentences for each word and its base word. Notice how the prefixes change word meanings.

■ Choose twelve word cards from those provided by your teacher. Write the words and say each word. Write sentences for each word and its base word. Notice how the suffixes change word meanings.

Word Work

Long *e* and Long *o* Vowels

15 min.

You will need
• Teacher-made word cards • paper • pencil

● Choose nine word cards from those provided by your teacher. Say each word. Write your words. Circle the long *e* or long *o* vowel sound in each word.

▲ Choose twelve word cards from those provided by your teacher and write each word. Say each word. Circle the long *e* or long *o* vowel sound in each word. Next to each word, write a rhyming word.

■ Choose twelve word cards from those provided by your teacher and write each word. Say each word. Next to each word, write a rhyming word. Write a funny four- or eight-line poem using some of the words.

Word Work

Schwa

You will need

15 min.

- Teacher-made word cards
- paper
- pencil

● Choose seven word cards from those provided by your teacher. List the words. Say each word, listening for the schwa sound. Think of other words that have the schwa sound. Add the words to your list.

▲ Choose nine word cards from those provided by your teacher and list the words. Say each word and listen for the schwa sound. Add other words that have the schwa sound to your list.

■ Choose twelve word cards from those provided by your teacher and list the words. Say each word, noticing the schwa sound. Add other words that have the schwa sound to your list.

Words with Long *e*

You will need

15 min.

- Teacher-made word cards
- paper
- pencil

● Choose eight word cards from those provided by your teacher. Say each word. Make a three-column chart with headings *ie, ey,* and *y.* Notice which letters form the long *e* sound. Fill in your chart with the words.

▲ Choose ten word cards from those provided by your teacher and say each word. Make a three-column chart with headings *ie, ey,* and *y.* Notice which letters form the long *e* sound. Fill in your chart with the words.

■ Make a three-column chart with headings *ie, ey,* and *y.* Choose twelve word card from those provided by your teacher and say each word. Fill in the chart by noting which letters form each word's long *e* sound.

Word Work

Related Words

You will need

15 min.

- Teacher-made word cards
- paper
- pencil

● Choose four pairs of related word cards from those provided by your teacher. Write the words. Say each word. Think of other pairs of related words you know. Add them to your list.

▲ Choose six pairs of related word cards from those provided by your teacher and write the words. Say each word. Think of other related word pairs you know and add them to your list.

■ Choose eight pairs of related word cards from those provided by your teacher and write the words. Say each word. Think of other related word pairs that you know and add them to your list.

Word Work

Words with Long *u*

15 min.

You will need
- Teacher-made word cards
- paper
- pencil

● Choose six word cards from those provided by your teacher. Write the words. Say each word. Circle the letter or letters that form the long *u* sound. Write a rhyming word next to each word on the list.

▲ Choose nine word cards from those provided by your teacher and write the words. Say each word. Circle the letter or letters that form the long *u* sound in each word. Write a rhyming word next to each word.

■ Choose twelve word cards from those provided by your teacher and write the words. Say each word. Circle the letter or letters that form the long *u* sound in each word. Write a rhyming word next to each word.

Word Work

Greek and Latin Prefixes

15 min.

You will need

- Teacher-made word cards
- paper
- pencil

● Choose six word cards from those provided by your teacher. Group the words by their prefix. Write the words. Say each word. Write other words you know with these prefixes.

▲ Choose nine word cards from those provided by your teacher. Group the words by their prefixes. Write the words and say each word. Add other words you know that share these prefixes.

■ Choose twelve word cards from those provided by your teacher and group the words by their prefixes. Write the words and say each word. Add other words that share these prefixes.

Words with *-s* *-es* or *-ies*

15 min.

You will need
- Teacher-made word cards • paper • pencil

● Choose six word cards with plural words from those provided by your teacher. Write the words. Next to each plural word, write its singular form. Say each word. Add other plural words you know to the list.

▲ Choose nine word cards with plural words from those provided by your teacher and write the words. Next to each plural word, write its singular form. Say each word. Add other plural words you know to the list.

■ Choose twelve word cards from those provided by your teacher and write the words. Next to each plural word, write its singular form. Say each word. Add other words in their plural and singular forms to the list.

Word Work

Greek Word Parts

15 min.

You will need
- Teacher-made word cards
- paper
- pencils

● Choose four word cards from those provided by your teacher with different Greek word parts. Make a four-column chart. Use the word parts as headings. Say each word. Add other words you know with these word parts to the chart.

▲ Choose five word cards from those provided by your teacher with different Greek word parts. Make a five-column chart. Use the word parts as headings. Quietly say each word aloud. Add other words you know with these word parts to the chart.

■ Sort the word cards provided by your teacher by Greek word part. Make a chart using the word parts as headings. Say each word. Fill in the chart with the words. Add other words you know with these word parts.

Word Work

Irregular Plurals

You will need

15 min.

- Teacher-made word cards   • paper   • pencil

● Choose six word cards with irregular plural words from those provided by your teacher. Write the words. Next to each plural word, write its singular form. Say each word. Add other irregular plural words you know to the list.

▲ Choose nine word cards with irregular plural words from those provided by your teacher and write the words. Next to each plural word, write its singular form. Say each word. Add other irregular plural words you know to the list.

■ Choose twelve word cards from those provided by your teacher and write the words. Next to each irregular plural word, write its singular form. Say each word. Add other words in their plural and singular forms to the list.

Word Work

Double Consonants

15 min.

You will need
- Teacher-made word cards
- paper
- pencil

● Choose six word cards from those provided by your teacher. Write the words and say each word. Think of other words with double consonants. Add the words to your list.

▲ Choose ten word cards from those provided by your teacher and write the words. Say each word. Add other words with double consonants to your list. Write a funny, four- or eight-line poem using some of the words.

■ Choose twelve word cards from those provided by your teacher and write the words. Say each word. Add other double consonant words to your list. Use the words in a funny, eight-line poem.

Word Work

Words with *ar* and *or*

15 min.

You will need
- Teacher-made word cards
- paper
- pencil

● Choose eight word cards from those provided by your teacher. Make a two-column chart with the headings *ar* and *or*. Write each word in the correct column. Add other words with *ar* or *or* to your chart. Say each word.

▲ Choose ten word cards from those provided by your teacher. Make a two-column chart with *ar* and *or* as headings. Write each word in the correct column. Add other words with *ar* or *or* to your chart. Say each word.

■ Choose twelve word cards from those provided by your teacher. Make a two-column chart with the headings *ar* and *or*. Write each word in the correct column. Add other words with *ar* or *or* to your chart. Say each word.

Word Work

Multisyllabic Words

15 min.

You will need
- Teacher-made word cards
- paper
- pencil

● Choose six word cards from those provided by your teacher. Write the words and say each word. Think of other multisyllabic words you know. Add them to your list.

▲ Choose nine word cards from those provided by your teacher and write the words. Say each word. Add other multisyllabic words you know to your list.

■ Choose twelve word cards from those provided by your teacher and write the words. Say each word. Add other multisyllabic words you know to your list.

Word Work

Consonant Pairs *ng, nk, ph,* and *wh*

15 min.

You will need
- Teacher-made word cards
- paper
- pencil

● Choose six word cards from those provided by your teacher. Write the words. Circle the consonant pairs in each word. Say each word. Add other words with consonant pairs *ng, nk, ph,* or *wh* to your list.

▲ Choose nine word cards from those provided by your teacher and write the words. Circle the consonant pairs in each word and say each word. Add other words with these consonant pairs to your list.

■ Choose twelve word cards from those provided by your teacher and write the words. Circle the consonant pairs in each word, and say each word. Add other words with these consonant pairs to your list.

Word Work

Prefixes *un-*, *dis-*, and *in-*

15 min.

You will need
- Teacher-made word cards
- paper
- pencil

● Choose three word cards from those provided by your teacher with each prefix: *un-*, *dis-* and *in-*. Write the words. Say each word. Circle the base word in each word.

▲ Choose four word cards from those provided by your teacher with each prefix: *un-*, *dis-* and *in*. Write the words and say each word. Circle the base word in each word.

■ Choose five word cards from those provided by your teacher with each prefix: *un-*, *dis-* and *in*. Write the words and say each word. Circle the base word in each word.

Word Work

Words with *-ear, -ir, -our,* and *-ur*

You will need   15 min.

• Teacher-made word cards   • paper   • pencil

● Choose nine word cards from those provided by your teacher. Make a four-column chart with letter combinations *-ear, -ir, -our,* and *-ur* as headings. Write the words in the correct columns. Say each word.

▲ Choose twelve word cards from those provided by your teacher. Make a four-column chart with letter combinations *-ear, -ir, -our,* and *-ur* as headings. Write the words in the correct columns. Say each word.

■ Choose fifteen word cards from those provided by your teacher. Make a four-column chart with letter combinations *-ear, -ir, -our,* and *-ur* as headings. Write the word cards in the correct columns. Say each word.

Word Work

Consonant Digraph /sh/

You will need

15 min.

- Teacher-made word cards
- paper
- pencil

● Choose six word cards from those provided by your teacher. Write your words in a list. Say each word aloud. Circle the letters in each word that form the /sh/ sound. Add other words with this sound to your list.

▲ Choose eight word cards from those provided by your teacher and write your words in a list. Say each word aloud. Circle the letters in each word that form the /sh/ sound. Add other words with this sound to your list.

■ Choose twelve word cards from those provided by your teacher and write your words in a list. Say each word aloud. Circle the letters in each word that form the /sh/ sound. Add other words with this sound to your list.

Word Work

Words with -ed and -ing

You will need

15 min.

• Teacher-made word cards • paper • pencil

● Choose seven word cards from those provided by your teacher. Make a three-column chart with headings *Base Word, -ed Added,* and *-ing Added.* Write your words in the correct column. Fill in your chart. Say each word.

▲ Choose ten word cards from those provided by your teacher. Make a three-column chart with headings *Base Word, -ed Added,* and *-ing Added.* Write your words in the correct column. Fill in your chart. Say each word.

■ Choose twelve word cards from those provided by your teacher. Make a three-column chart with headings *Base Word, -ed Added,* and *-ing Added.* Write your words in the correct column. Fill in your chart. Say each word.

Word Work

Words with Endings *-er* and *-ar*

You will need

15 min.

- Teacher-made word cards
- paper
- pencil

● Choose eight word cards from those provided by your teacher. Make a two-column chart with headings *Ends in -ar* and *Ends in -er*. Write each word in the correct column. Say each word aloud.

▲ Choose ten word cards from those provided by your teacher. Make a two-column chart with headings *Ends in -ar* and *Ends in -er*. Write each word in the correct column and say each word aloud.

■ Choose twelve word cards from those provided by your teacher. Make a two-column chart with headings *Ends in -ar* and *Ends in -er*. Write each word in the correct column and quietly say each word aloud.

Word Work

Homophones

You will need

15 min.

- Teacher-made word cards
- paper
- pencil

● Choose five pairs of homophones from the word cards provided by your teacher. Write your words in a list. Say each word aloud. Think of other homophones you know. Add them to your list.

▲ Choose six teacher-provided word cards that are not homophone pairs. List each word on paper. Say each word aloud. Write a homophone next to each word.

■ Choose ten teacher-provided word cards that are not homophone pairs. Say each word aloud. List each word on paper and write a homophone next to it. Add other homophones to the list.

Word Work

Final Syllable Patterns

15 min.

You will need
• Teacher-made word cards • paper • pencil

● Choose six word cards from those provided by your teacher. Group your words by final syllable sound. Write the words in a list. Say each word aloud. Write a rhyming word next to each word on your list.

▲ Choose eight word cards from those provided by your teacher and group your words by final syllable sound. Write the words in a list and say each word aloud. Write a rhyming word next to each word on your list.

■ Choose ten word cards from those provided by your teacher and group your words by final syllable sound. List the words and say each word. Use some of the words to write a funny, four-line rhyming poem.

Word Work

Vowel Sound in *Shout*

15 min.

You will need
- Teacher-made word cards
- paper
- pencil

● Choose eight word cards from those provided by your teacher. Say each word aloud. Make a two-column chart with headings *ow* and *ou.* Write the words in the correct column. Write a rhyming word for each word.

▲ Choose ten word cards from those provided by your teacher and say each word aloud. Make a two-column chart with headings *ow* and *ou.* Write the words in the correct column. Write a rhyming word for each word.

■ Choose twelve word cards from those provided by your teacher and say each word. Group your words by the vowels that form the sound in *shout.* Write the words in a list. Next to each word, write a rhyming word.

Word Work

Contractions

15 min.

You will need
- Teacher-made word cards
- paper
- pencil

● Choose six word cards from those provided by your teacher. Write the words in a list. Say each word aloud. Think of other contractions that you know. Add the words to your list.

▲ Choose nine word cards from those provided by your teacher and write the words in a list. Say each word aloud. Think of other contractions that you know and add them to your list.

■ Choose twelve word cards from those provided by your teacher and write the words in a list. Say each word aloud. Add other contractions that you know to your list.

Word Work

Compound Words

15 min.

You will need
- magazines
- paper
- pencils

● Use the magazines to find five compound words. Write your words in a list. Say each word aloud. Draw a line between the two words that make up the compound word.

▲ Use the magazines to find eight compound words. Write your words in a list. Say each word aloud. Add other compound words you know to the list.

■ Using the magazines or words you already know, make a list of twelve compound words. Say each word aloud. Next to each compound word, write a rhyming word.

Word Work

Possessives

You will need
15 min.
- Teacher-made word cards • paper • pencil

● Choose five word cards from those provided by your teacher. Write the words in a list. Say each word. Next to each word, write whether it is *singular possessive* or *plural possessive*.

▲ Choose seven word cards from those provided by your teacher and write the words. Say each word. Next to each word, write whether it is *singular possessive* or *plural possessive*.

■ Choose nine word cards from those provided by your teacher and write the words in a list. Say each word. Next to each word, write whether it is *singular possessive* or *plural possessive*.

Get Fluent

Practice Fluent Reading

15 min.

You will need
- Leveled Readers

● Work with a partner. Choose a leveled reader from those provided by your teacher. As you read, look at how words are grouped into phrases. Read with appropriate phrasing, using punctuation as a guide. Provide feedback to your partner.

▲ Work with a partner. Choose a leveled reader from those provided by your teacher. As you read, look at how words are grouped into phrases. Read with appropriate phrasing, using punctuation as a guide. Provide feedback to your partner.

■ Work with a partner. Choose a leveled reader from those provided by your teacher. As you read, look at how words are grouped into phrases. Read with appropriate phrasing, using punctuation as a guide. Provide feedback to your partner.

Get Fluent

Practice Fluent Reading

15 min.

You will need
- Leveled Readers

● Work with a partner. Choose a leveled reader from those provided by your teacher. As you read, look at how words are grouped into phrases. Read with appropriate phrasing, using punctuation as a guide. Provide feedback to your partner.

▲ Work with a partner. Choose a leveled reader from those provided by your teacher. As you read, look at how words are grouped into phrases. Read with appropriate phrasing, using punctuation as a guide. Provide feedback to your partner.

■ Work with a partner. Choose a leveled reader from those provided by your teacher. As you read, look at how words are grouped into phrases. Read with appropriate phrasing, using punctuation as a guide. Provide feedback to your partner.

Practice Fluent Reading

15 min.

You will need
- Leveled Readers

● Work with a partner. Choose a leveled reader from those provided by your teacher. Take turns reading a page from the book. Use the words and punctuation to help you read with correct expression. Provide feedback to your partner.

▲ Work with a partner. Choose a leveled reader from those provided by your teacher. Take turns reading a page from the book. Use the words and punctuation to help you read with correct expression. Provide feedback to your partner.

■ Work with a partner. Choose a leveled reader from those provided by your teacher. Take turns reading a page from the book. Use the words and punctuation to help you read with correct expression. Provide feedback to your partner.

Get Fluent

Practice Fluent Reading

15 min.

You will need
- Leveled Readers

● Work with a partner. Choose a leveled reader from those provided by your teacher. As you read, look at how words are grouped into phrases. Read with appropriate phrasing, using punctuation as a guide. Provide feedback to your partner.

▲ Work with a partner. Choose a leveled reader from those provided by your teacher. As you read, look at how words are grouped into phrases. Read with appropriate phrasing, using punctuation as a guide. Provide feedback to your partner.

■ Work with a partner. Choose a leveled reader from those provided by your teacher. As you read, look at how words are grouped into phrases. Read with appropriate phrasing, using punctuation as a guide. Provide feedback to your partner.

Get Fluent

Practice Fluent Reading

15 min.

You will need
- Leveled Readers

● Work with a partner. Choose a leveled reader from those provided by your teacher. As you read, look at how words are grouped into phrases. Read with appropriate phrasing, using punctuation as a guide. Provide feedback to your partner.

▲ Work with a partner. Choose a leveled reader from those provided by your teacher. As you read, look at how words are grouped into phrases. Read with appropriate phrasing, using punctuation as a guide. Provide feedback to your partner.

■ Work with a partner. Choose a leveled reader from those provided by your teacher. As you read, look at how words are grouped into phrases. Read with appropriate phrasing, using punctuation as a guide. Provide feedback to your partner.

Get Fluent

Practice Fluent Reading

15 min.

You will need
- Leveled Readers

● Work with a partner. Choose a leveled reader from those provided by your teacher. Take turns reading a page from the book. Use the words and punctuation to help you read with correct expression. Provide feedback to your partner.

▲ Work with a partner. Choose a leveled reader from those provided by your teacher. Take turns reading a page from the book. Use the words and punctuation to help you read with correct expression. Provide feedback to your partner.

■ Work with a partner. Choose a leveled reader from those provided by your teacher. Take turns reading a page from the book. Use the words and punctuation to help you read with correct expression. Provide feedback to your partner.

Get Fluent

Practice Fluent Reading

15 min.

You will need
- Leveled Readers

● Work with a partner. Choose a leveled reader from those provided by your teacher. Take turns reading a page from the book. Use the words and punctuation to help you read with correct expression. Provide feedback to your partner.

▲ Work with a partner. Choose a leveled reader from those provided by your teacher. Take turns reading a page from the book. Use the words and punctuation to help you read with correct expression. Provide feedback to your partner.

■ Work with a partner. Choose a leveled reader from those provided by your teacher. Take turns reading a page from the book. Use the words and punctuation to help you read with correct expression. Provide feedback to your partner.

Get Fluent

Practice Fluent Reading

15 min.

You will need
- Leveled Readers

● Work with a partner. Choose a leveled reader from those provided by your teacher. Take turns reading a page from the book. Use the words and punctuation to help you read with correct expression. Provide feedback to your partner.

▲ Work with a partner. Choose a leveled reader from those provided by your teacher. Take turns reading a page from the book. Use the words and punctuation to help you read with correct expression. Provide feedback to your partner.

■ Work with a partner. Choose a leveled reader from those provided by your teacher. Take turns reading a page from the book. Use the words and punctuation to help you read with correct expression. Provide feedback to your partner.

Get Fluent

Practice Fluent Reading

15 min.

You will need
- Leveled Readers

● Work with a partner. Choose a leveled reader from those provided by your teacher. As you read, look at how words are grouped into phrases. Read with appropriate phrasing, using punctuation as a guide. Provide feedback to your partner.

▲ Work with a partner. Choose a leveled reader from those provided by your teacher. As you read, look at how words are grouped into phrases. Read with appropriate phrasing, using punctuation as a guide. Provide feedback to your partner.

■ Work with a partner. Choose a leveled reader from those provided by your teacher. As you read, look at how words are grouped into phrases. Read with appropriate phrasing, using punctuation as a guide. Provide feedback to your partner.

Get Fluent

Practice Fluent Reading

15 min.

You will need
• Leveled Readers

● Work with a partner. Choose a leveled reader from those provided by your teacher. Take turns reading a page from the book. Use the words and punctuation to help you read with correct expression. Provide feedback to your partner.

▲ Work with a partner. Choose a leveled reader from those provided by your teacher. Take turns reading a page from the book. Use the words and punctuation to help you read with correct expression. Provide feedback to your partner.

■ Work with a partner. Choose a leveled reader from those provided by your teacher. Take turns reading a page from the book. Use the words and punctuation to help you read with correct expression. Provide feedback to your partner.

Get Fluent

Practice Fluent Reading

15 min.

You will need
- Leveled Readers

● Work with a partner. Choose a leveled reader from those provided by your teacher. Take turns reading a page from the book. Use the words and punctuation to help you read with correct expression. Provide feedback to your partner.

▲ Work with a partner. Choose a leveled reader from those provided by your teacher. Take turns reading a page from the book. Use the words and punctuation to help you read with correct expression. Provide feedback to your partner.

■ Work with a partner. Choose a leveled reader from those provided by your teacher. Take turns reading a page from the book. Use the words and punctuation to help you read with correct expression. Provide feedback to your partner.

Practice Fluent Reading

You will need
- Leveled Readers

15 min.

● Work with a partner. Choose a leveled reader from those provided by your teacher. Take turns reading a page from the book. Raise and lower your voice to help you read with expression. Provide feedback to your partner.

▲ Work with a partner. Choose a leveled reader from those provided by your teacher. Take turns reading a page from the book. Raise and lower your voice to help you read with expression. Provide feedback to your partner.

■ Work with a partner. Choose a leveled reader from those provided by your teacher. Take turns reading a page from the book. Raise and lower your voice to help you read with expression. Provide feedback to your partner.

Get Fluent

Practice Fluent Reading

15 min.

You will need
• Leveled Readers

● Work with a partner. Choose a leveled reader from those provided by your teacher. Take turns reading a page from the book. Think about the topic of the book. As you read, try to read with appropriate rate and accuracy. Provide feedback to your partner.

▲ Work with a partner. Choose a leveled reader from those provided by your teacher. Take turns reading a page from the book. Think about the topic of the book. As you read, try to read with appropriate rate and accuracy. Provide feedback to your partner.

■ Work with a partner. Choose a leveled reader from those provided by your teacher. Take turns reading a page from the book. Think about the topic of the book. As you read, try to read with appropriate rate and accuracy. Provide feedback to your partner.

Get Fluent

Practice Fluent Reading

You will need

15 min.

- Leveled Readers

● Work with a partner. Choose a leveled reader from those provided by your teacher. Take turns reading a page from the book. Use the words and punctuation to help you read with correct expression. Provide feedback to your partner.

▲ Work with a partner. Choose a leveled reader from those provided by your teacher. Take turns reading a page from the book. Use the words and punctuation to help you read with correct expression. Provide feedback to your partner.

■ Work with a partner. Choose a leveled reader from those provided by your teacher. Take turns reading a page from the book. Use the words and punctuation to help you read with correct expression. Provide feedback to your partner.

Get Fluent

Practice Fluent Reading

15 min.

You will need
- Leveled Readers

● Work with a partner. Choose a leveled reader from those provided by your teacher. As you read, look at how words are grouped into phrases. Read with appropriate phrasing, using punctuation as a guide. Provide feedback to your partner.

▲ Work with a partner. Choose a leveled reader from those provided by your teacher. As you read, look at how words are grouped into phrases. Read with appropriate phrasing, using punctuation as a guide. Provide feedback to your partner.

■ Work with a partner. Choose a leveled reader from those provided by your teacher. As you read, look at how words are grouped into phrases. Read with appropriate phrasing, using punctuation as a guide. Provide feedback to your partner.

Get Fluent

Practice Fluent Reading

15 min.

You will need
• Leveled Readers

● Work with a partner. Choose a leveled reader from those provided by your teacher. Take turns reading a page from the book. Use the words and punctuation to help you read with correct expression. Provide feedback to your partner.

▲ Work with a partner. Choose a leveled reader from those provided by your teacher. Take turns reading a page from the book. Use the words and punctuation to help you read with correct expression. Provide feedback to your partner.

■ Work with a partner. Choose a leveled reader from those provided by your teacher. Take turns reading a page from the book. Use the words and punctuation to help you read with correct expression. Provide feedback to your partner.

Get Fluent

Practice Fluent Reading

15 min.

You will need
- Leveled Readers

● Work with a partner. Choose a leveled reader from those provided by your teacher. Take turns reading a page from the book. Raise and lower your voice to help you read with expression. Provide feedback to your partner.

▲ Work with a partner. Choose a leveled reader from those provided by your teacher. Take turns reading a page from the book. Raise and lower your voice to help you read with expression. Provide feedback to your partner.

■ Work with a partner. Choose a leveled reader from those provided by your teacher. Take turns reading a page from the book. Raise and lower your voice to help you read with expression. Provide feedback to your partner.

Get Fluent

Practice Fluent Reading

15 min.

You will need
• Leveled Readers

● Work with a partner. Choose a leveled reader from those provided by your teacher. Take turns reading a page from the book. Use the words and punctuation to help you read with correct expression. Provide feedback to your partner.

▲ Work with a partner. Choose a leveled reader from those provided by your teacher. Take turns reading a page from the book. Use the words and punctuation to help you read with correct expression. Provide feedback to your partner.

■ Work with a partner. Choose a leveled reader from those provided by your teacher. Take turns reading a page from the book. Use the words and punctuation to help you read with correct expression. Provide feedback to your partner.

Get Fluent

Practice Fluent Reading

15 min.

You will need

- Leveled Readers

● Work with a partner. Choose a leveled reader from those provided by your teacher. Take turns reading a page from the book. As you read, change your tone of voice to read with expression and emotion. Provide feedback to your partner.

▲ Work with a partner. Choose a leveled reader from those provided by your teacher. Take turns reading a page from the book. As you read, change your tone of voice to read with expression and emotion. Provide feedback to your partner.

■ Work with a partner. Choose a leveled reader from those provided by your teacher. Take turns reading a page from the book. As you read, change your tone of voice to read with expression and emotion. Provide feedback to your partner.

Get Fluent

Practice Fluent Reading

15 min.

You will need
- Leveled Readers

● Work with a partner. Choose a leveled reader from those provided by your teacher. Take turns reading a page from the book. Look at how words are grouped into phrases. Punctuation can help you read with appropriate phrasing. Provide feedback to your partner.

▲ Work with a partner. Choose a leveled reader from those provided by your teacher. Take turns reading a page from the book. Look at how words are grouped into phrases. Punctuation can help you read with appropriate phrasing. Provide feedback to your partner.

■ Work with a partner. Choose a leveled reader from those provided by your teacher. Take turns reading a page from the book. Look at how words are grouped into phrases. Punctuation can help you read with appropriate phrasing. Provide feedback to your partner.

Get Fluent

Practice Fluent Reading

15 min.

You will need
- Leveled Readers

● Work with a partner. Choose a leveled reader from those provided by your teacher. Take turns reading a page from the book. Read as accurately as you can. Use punctuation clues to help you read with accuracy. Provide feedback to your partner.

▲ Work with a partner. Choose a leveled reader from those provided by your teacher. Take turns reading a page from the book. Read as accurately as you can. Use punctuation clues to help you read with accuracy. Provide feedback to your partner.

■ Work with a partner. Choose a leveled reader from those provided by your teacher. Take turns reading a page from the book. Read as accurately as you can. Use punctuation clues to help you read with accuracy. Provide feedback to your partner.

Get Fluent

Practice Fluent Reading

15 min.

You will need
- Leveled Readers

● Work with a partner. Choose a leveled reader from those provided by your teacher. Take turns reading a page from the book. Look at how words are grouped into phrases. Punctuation can help you read with appropriate phrasing. Provide feedback to your partner.

▲ Work with a partner. Choose a leveled reader from those provided by your teacher. Take turns reading a page from the book. Look at how words are grouped into phrases. Punctuation can help you read with appropriate phrasing. Provide feedback to your partner.

■ Work with a partner. Choose a leveled reader from those provided by your teacher. Take turns reading a page from the book. Look at how words are grouped into phrases. Punctuation can help you read with appropriate phrasing. Provide feedback to your partner.

Get Fluent

Practice Fluent Reading

15 min.

You will need
- Leveled Readers

● Work with a partner. Choose a leveled reader from those provided by your teacher. As you read, look at how words are grouped into phrases. Read with appropriate phrasing, using punctuation as a guide. Provide feedback to your partner.

▲ Work with a partner. Choose a leveled reader from those provided by your teacher. As you read, look at how words are grouped into phrases. Read with appropriate phrasing, using punctuation as a guide. Provide feedback to your partner.

■ Work with a partner. Choose a leveled reader from those provided by your teacher. As you read, look at how words are grouped into phrases. Read with appropriate phrasing, using punctuation as a guide. Provide feedback to your partner.

Get Fluent

Practice Fluent Reading

15 min.

You will need
- Leveled Readers

● Work with a partner. Choose a leveled reader from those provided by your teacher. Take turns reading a page from the book. Use the words and punctuation to help you read with correct expression. Provide feedback to your partner.

▲ Work with a partner. Choose a leveled reader from those provided by your teacher. Take turns reading a page from the book. Use the words and punctuation to help you read with correct expression. Provide feedback to your partner.

■ Work with a partner. Choose a leveled reader from those provided by your teacher. Take turns reading a page from the book. Use the words and punctuation to help you read with correct expression. Provide feedback to your partner.

Practice Fluent Reading

You will need
- Leveled Readers

15 min.

● Work with a partner. Choose a leveled reader from those provided by your teacher. Take turns reading a page from the book. Raise and lower your voice to help you read with expression. Provide feedback to your partner.

▲ Work with a partner. Choose a leveled reader from those provided by your teacher. Take turns reading a page from the book. Raise and lower your voice to help you read with expression. Provide feedback to your partner.

■ Work with a partner. Choose a leveled reader from those provided by your teacher. Take turns reading a page from the book. Raise and lower your voice to help you read with expression. Provide feedback to your partner.

Get Fluent

Practice Fluent Reading

15 min.

You will need
- Leveled Readers

● Work with a partner. Choose a leveled reader from those provided by your teacher. Take turns reading a page from the book. Think about the topic of the book. As you read, match your rate to what you are reading. Provide feedback to your partner.

▲ Work with a partner. Choose a leveled reader from those provided by your teacher. Take turns reading a page from the book. Think about the topic of the book. As you read, match your rate to what you are reading. Provide feedback to your partner.

■ Work with a partner. Choose a leveled reader from those provided by your teacher. Take turns reading a page from the book. Think about the topic of the book. As you read, match your rate to what you are reading. Provide feedback to your partner.

Practice Fluent Reading

You will need

15 min.

- Leveled Readers

● Work with a partner. Choose a leveled reader from those provided by your teacher. Take turns reading a page from the book. Raise and lower your voice to help you read with expression. Provide feedback to your partner.

▲ Work with a partner. Choose a leveled reader. from those provided by your teacher Take turns reading a page from the book. Raise and lower your voice to help you read with expression. Provide feedback to your partner.

■ Work with a partner. Choose a leveled reader from those provided by your teacher. Take turns reading a page from the book. Raise and lower your voice to help you read with expression. Provide feedback to your partner.

Get Fluent

Practice Fluent Reading

You will need
- Leveled Readers

15 min.

● Work with a partner. Choose a leveled reader from those provided by your teacher. Take turns reading a page from the book. Look at how words are grouped into phrases. Punctuation can help you read with appropriate phrasing. Provide feedback to your partner.

▲ Work with a partner. Choose a leveled reader from those provided by your teacher. Take turns reading a page from the book. Look at how words are grouped into phrases. Punctuation can help you read with appropriate phrasing. Provide feedback to your partner.

■ Work with a partner. Choose a leveled reader from those provided by your teacher. Take turns reading a page from the book. Look at how words are grouped into phrases. Punctuation can help you read with appropriate phrasing. Provide feedback to your partner.

Practice Fluent Reading

You will need
- Leveled Readers

15 min.

● Work with a partner. Choose a leveled reader from those provided by your teacher. As you read, look at how words are grouped into phrases. Read with appropriate phrasing, using punctuation as a guide. Provide feedback to your partner.

▲ Work with a partner. Choose a leveled reader from those provided by your teacher. As you read, look at how words are grouped into phrases. Read with appropriate phrasing, using punctuation as a guide. Provide feedback to your partner.

■ Work with a partner. Choose a leveled reader from those provided by your teacher. As you read, look at how words are grouped into phrases. Read with appropriate phrasing, using punctuation as a guide. Provide feedback to your partner.

Get Fluent

Practice Fluent Reading

15 min.

You will need
- Leveled Readers

● Work with a partner. Choose a leveled reader from those provided by your teacher. Take turns reading a page from the book. Use the words and punctuation to help you read with correct expression. Provide feedback to your partner.

▲ Work with a partner. Choose a leveled reader from those provided by your teacher. Take turns reading a page from the book. Use the words and punctuation to help you read with correct expression. Provide feedback to your partner.

■ Work with a partner. Choose a leveled reader from those provided by your teacher. Take turns reading a page from the book. Use the words and punctuation to help you read with correct expression. Provide feedback to your partner.